a gift of
happiness

a gift of
happiness

Gill Farrer-Halls

With illustrations from the
collection of Robert Beer

Andrews McMeel
Publishing

Kansas City

First published by MQ Publications Limited
12 The Ivories, 6–8 Northampton Street
London N1 2HY

Copyright © 2004 MQ Publications Limited
Text © 2004 Gill Farrer-Halls
Illustrations © 2004 Robert Beer

Series editor: Abi Rowsell
Design: Yvonne Dedman

ISBN: 0 7407 4060 1
Library of Congress Control Number: on file
03 04 05 06 07 PAR 10 9 8 7 6 5 4 3 2 1

Attention: Schools and Businesses
Andrews McMeel books are available at quantity discounts with bulk purchase for educational, business,
or sales promotional use. For information, please write to: Special Sales Department, Andrews McMeel
Publishing, 4520 Main Street, Kansas City, Missouri 64111.

contents

introduction

The Sanskrit word *karma* is now part of the English language. Expressions such as "bad karma" and "good karma" are commonly used these days. Jokes such as "Your karma ran over my dogma" are amusing, but don't make sense, and expose the fact that most of us native English speakers do not have much understanding of the true meaning of the word. We tend to use this term to describe a mystical fate or fortune, which is not entirely incorrect but does miss the full meaning and subtle complexities of what karma is and how it works in our lives. This book takes a look at what karma really means.

Firstly, note that the original texts of Buddhism were written in Sanskrit and Pali. Karma is called "kamma" in Pali, the Indic language used in the canonical books of Buddhism. You will see both versions in the quotations used in this book, but they mean the same thing.

The law of karma

Sometimes people refer to the law of karma as a natural and inescapable law of the universe. While integral to Buddhist teachings, including those about compassion and wisdom, essentially karma means action, although this is a general definition.

More precisely, Buddhists say that karma refers to actions that are willed or meant—that is, those that have intention behind them. However, even if we do something instinctively, without thinking about it, there is still some level of unconscious intention at work.

Therefore, all of our actions can create karma. Their effects can vary between being powerful or weak depending on different conditions and situations. Traditional Buddhist texts state that Buddhas, or people who have become enlightened, are the only ones whose actions are perfectly "pure" and no longer generate any karma.

Mental, verbal, and bodily karma

Karma has a threefold classification:

1. mental karma—created by the mind and thoughts,
2. verbal karma—created by speech, and
3. bodily karma—caused by physical actions.

Mental karma is the most significant of the three because it gives rise to, and is the origin of, the other two types of karma. We think before we speak or physically do something, however briefly, and our thoughts influence what we say and do.

Furthermore, two types of karmic actions are described here: ones that are positive, skillful, beneficial, and also good, and those that are negative, unskillful, harmful, and ultimately bad.

Ten negative actions that create bad karma

There are ten main negative actions that create bad karma: the three physical acts of killing, stealing, and sexual misconduct (including acts such as adultery); followed by the four negative acts of speech, i.e., lying, saying things to harm others or cause conflict between them, using harsh language such as swearing, and idle gossip; and ending with the three mental negative acts of covetousness, thinking ill of people, and holding wrong views, such as not understanding that anger causes suffering.

Ten positive actions that create good karma

These involve, first, giving up all negative actions, as noted before, and then cultivating their positive opposites. The three physical virtues are protecting life, being generous to others, and responsible sexual behavior. The four positive acts of speech include being truthful, creating harmony and reconciliation among others, talking pleasantly, and having useful conversations. The three mental virtues are being content with what one has, being kind to others, and developing conviction that what the Buddha taught is beneficial.

Negative karma

Negative karma arises from actions that are driven by ignorance or delusion; hatred, aversion, or anger; or greed, attachment, or avarice. These are called the Three Poisons in Buddhism, and are the qualities that keep us trapped in samsara, the cycle of birth and rebirth, which we only escape by reaching enlightenment.

Positive karma

Positive karma arises from actions that are not rooted in ignorance, hatred, or greed. Although we could say positive karma arises from wisdom, love, and renunciation, it is traditional to describe the positive qualities as directly opposite to the Three Poisons, because this reminds us of what they are and to try to avoid them.

Three stages must occur for an action to be complete:

1. the motivation to perform the action,
2. the successful fulfillment of the action, and
3. the satisfaction of completing the action.

If only one or two stages are fulfilled, the karma created is less, while a completed action generates greater karmic consequences. For example, if you mistakenly squash an insect and are sorry to have killed it, only the action itself has occurred; there was no intention or satisfaction in the act.

The karmic consequences are, therefore, less than if you deliberately jumped on the insect and were happy to have successfully killed it.

The law of cause and effect

Karma is also called the law of cause and effect. This means that every action, however tiny or seemingly insignificant, creates a cause for an eventual result, which is called the fruit of the action. These consequences are complex and influenced by hundreds of little factors during our lives, and through many different lifetimes, that intermingle. Because of this, we often cannot see clearly how karma operates.

Karmic fruition may be
experienced in this lifetime,
in the next lifetime,
or in other, future lives.

Karmic fruition

Most human actions create karmic consequences that are not experienced immediately but will definitely be experienced later.

The Buddhist scriptures say that the majority of our actions will bear fruit in future lives. A kind, generous, honest person who suffers in this life can rest assured he or she will experience the positive karmic consequences of his or her good actions in a later life. Someone behaving in ways that cause suffering for others, but enjoying a happy life, will suffer the consequences of the negative behavior in a later life.

Karma and rebirth

Karma and rebirth are deeply interlinked. What exactly is rebirth? Buddhism considers that only our most subtle consciousness goes from one life to the next. The individual person, both personality and characteristics, is extinguished at death. This subtle consciousness carries with it all the karma created in the life just finished, together with any karma from previous lives that has not yet come to fruition. These karmic imprints determine the quality of the next life, while some of the karma carried over will also come to fruition in the next life when it meets the appropriate conditions.

Certain behavior creates specific karmic consequences

A person who easily finds prosperity in this life may have created the cause by being generous in a previous existence. Someone who dies young in this life might have failed to protect others in a previous life.

Beauty could be the result of pure, ethical behavior in a past life, while people who are not taken seriously in this life may have created the cause by lying in a past existence. These examples illustrate how karma is linked with ethical, responsible behavior—we reap what we sow.

Black and white

Karma is classified according to its results. The first category is called

- **black** karma, **black** result

and includes all harmful actions of body, speech, and mind.

- white karma, white result

incorporates all nonharmful and virtuous actions.

- **black** and white karma,

  black and white result

includes actions that are partly harmful, partly not. For example, telling a lie in order not to hurt someone's feelings. Although the intention is positive, the act itself is not, so the karmic consequences will be mixed.

The last category needs more explanation. This is:

- karma that is neither **black** nor white,
  a result that is neither **black** nor white.

This arises when our underlying intention is to transcend the other kinds of karma altogether by trying to become enlightened, the ultimate goal of Buddhism. The purpose of practicing Buddhism is to avoid suffering and find happiness. This may make us feel that creating karma that brings happiness as the result is the best thing to do.

However, Buddhism teaches us that everything is impermanent, so even if we create the causes of happiness, the resulting happiness cannot last forever. Sooner or later the karma that created happiness will be exhausted and we will experience suffering. Our highest aspiration is to transcend karma on our path toward enlightenment.

Rebirth

While some early Christian sects believed in a form of rebirth, it is quite a difficult concept for some Westerners to accommodate. Since people are born with certain talents, however, we can begin to understand how karma moves from one life to the next. People with outstanding musical talent, for example, often speak of how they felt as if they already knew how to play music when they first started. Similarly, Mozart learned how to play music very quickly at an early age and had an inner sense of harmony and rhythm.

The Noble Eightfold Path

Attaining enlightenment is not easy! It is a state in which one is completely free from desire for, and attachment to, things one likes, and also from aversion to, and hatred for, what one doesn't like.

To develop the conditions within which this state may arise, Buddhists follow the Buddha's Noble Eightfold Path, which is a guide to living in a manner that does not cause suffering to oneself or others. It was created to help people reach enlightenment.

Enlightenment is the total liberation from suffering that the Buddha discovered, also referred to as nirvana and awakening.

This explanation of karma makes one thing very clear:

We are responsible for
whatever occurs in our lives.

The Noble Eightfold Path

The Noble Eightfold Path comprises:
1. Right view
2. Right thought
3. Right speech
4. Right action
5. Right livelihood
6. Right effort
7. Right mindfulness
8. Right concentration

The person who has happiness, health, and success created the foundations for a pleasant life by performing positive actions in previous lives.

Those who suffer illness, poverty, and so forth, likewise created the causes for their unpleasant experiences by committing negative actions previously. Most people have a mixture of good and bad experiences throughout their lives, reflecting the varied karma they created in earlier lives. So, karma is not fatalistic. By consciously trying to act with wisdom, love, kindness, and compassion for others as much as possible, we create the karma for positive rebirths. Virtuous behavior will eventually lead us beyond karma altogether, to enlightenment.

Purification

So, can anything be done about all the negative karma that has been created over many different lifetimes? Obviously it would be preferable not to experience all the bad karmic results! There is a way to erase some of our negative karma— purification. This requires understanding that you have behaved badly in the past and that you must take full responsibility for this behavior. Then you must sincerely regret and repent your negative actions and promise yourself to try not to behave badly again. Finally, try to perform only positive, virtuous actions from now on.

Just as musical talent may be the karmic result of musical training in an earlier life, behavioral patterns can also be karmic results. For example, if someone gets angry easily, this may be seen as a karmic consequence of previous angry behavior that the person now has the opportunity to purify. The person needs to try hard not to give in to the impulse to be angry, by reflecting that anger will create more negative karma and further intensify the habit of growing angry. While not easy, this is definitely worth attempting in order to avoid harming oneself and others in the present and in future lives.

That is a very brief introduction to karma. The following chapters examine in greater depth how karma operates and affects our lives. Practical suggestions and advice on how to generate good karma and avoid bad karma, will be offered, along with some inspiring quotations.

Once the profound nature
of karma is properly understood,
a path that can lead
to a happier life
may be discovered.

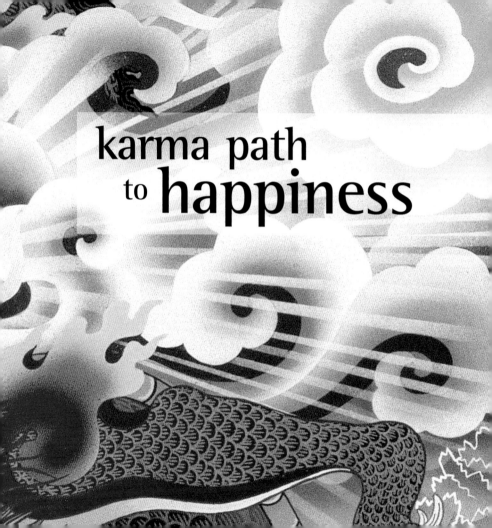

karma path
to happiness

Everyone wants to be happy
and to avoid suffering and dissatisfaction.
This is a universal truth
that does not depend on
nationality, age, wealth, gender,
or any other personal factor.

This truth also extends to animals. Although animals cannot speak to us, we know that a dog shivering with cold in the rain, waiting for its owner to come home and let it indoors to sit by the fire, wants to avoid the suffering of being cold and wet and hopes for the happiness of being warm and dry. Observations such as these support the theory that all beings everywhere want happiness and do not want suffering.

Because we want to be happy, we spend much of our lives trying to find objects and experiences that we imagine will make us happy. Many of us dedicate our lives to the endless pursuit of happiness and the avoidance of suffering. We work toward acquiring a nice home, a satisfying career, a loving partner, children, vacations, and so forth. However, no sooner do we satisfy our desires than we want more new, different things to keep us happy. Therefore,

all of our activities and worldly

pursuits are continuously motivated

by the desire for happiness

and the wish to avoid suffering.

WHITE MANJUSHRI

White Manjushri, the bodhisattva of wisdom, surrounded by six
of his manifestations, and with the longevity bodhisattva
Amitayus above.

This may seem rather obvious to many people, who might ask,

> What is the purpose of life,
> if it is not to find happiness?

So, because the wish for happiness is everyone's major preoccupation, it is a good idea to examine the causes of happiness and suffering to ensure we can fulfill our quest as successfully as possible.

An understanding of karma can be beneficial. As mentioned in the introduction, karma is known as the law of cause and effect. Karma explains how and why certain actions of body, speech, and mind cause certain effects and results.

When you clearly understand which of your actions will cause an effect of happiness and which actions cause suffering, then you know how to find happiness and avoid suffering.

If you want to find happiness, you must first eliminate the causes of suffering. Conversely, if you want to avoid suffering, you must cultivate the causes of happiness.

The first thing you need to determine is what causes happiness and suffering in the first place. Look at what you think makes you happy. Desires endlessly arise in the mind and body; we want new clothes, tasty meals, sexual gratification, and so on. We often take for granted that continually satisfying all of our desires will make us happy. However, once a desire is satisfied, the object of desire no longer brings happiness.

Desire does not bring happiness

Even the fulfillment of desires can turn into a source of dissatisfaction. For instance, when we go on vacation to relax, before long we grow bored and want to go home. Other desires continue to arise, no matter how often we gratify them. Therefore, satisfying our desires does not bring authentic happiness, merely temporary gratification.

When we do not have the things we desire, we crave them endlessly. This causes suffering. Likewise, when we have things or experiences we don't want, we get caught up in negative thoughts about how much we dislike the situation, and this aversion causes suffering.

When we do obtain the thing we desired, we are satisfied for a while, but before long we are bored with our new possession, or the effect of a pleasant experience wears off so we want to repeat it. Desire then arises again, and while it remains unfilled we are dissatisfied or suffering. Therefore we can conclude that satisfying our

desires does not cause real, lasting happiness. It simply keeps us trapped in an endless cycle of desire and dissatisfaction.

Real, lasting happiness arises from eliminating desire for the things we like and aversion to things we don't like. This doesn't mean that it is wrong or bad to want to have nice things, nor should we turn away from them if they come our way. We should certainly enjoy the good things that come our way—for as long as they last.

However, we do need to realize that desire itself is the obstacle that prevents us from finding true

GREEN TARA

Detail of a copy of a fourteenth-century painting of Green Tara, showing her ornate jewelry.

happiness and that keeps us dissatisfied. Desire causes suffering. When we understand this, we can enjoy pleasant experiences and possessions, but not be obsessive about having them nor disappointed when they cease to give us pleasure. When unpleasant things arise, or we don't get what we want, we can try to accept things as they are, reflecting that all things are impermanent and that, sooner or later, our suffering will change.

All the happiness and suffering we experience has specific causes and arises as a result of our own actions. Every action of body, speech, and mind can cause a person to experience either happiness or suffering. The cause of happiness is positive, ethical, wholesome actions, and the cause of suffering is negative, unwholesome, immoral actions. We have created the karma for all our experiences ourselves; there is no one to blame if we are experiencing suffering and no one to be grateful to if we are experiencing happiness. However, we should be thankful to Buddhist and other spiritual teachers for showing us how to discover real happiness, and be grateful for the kindness of others.

The operation of karma is not simple; it is extraordinarily complex. We cannot simply point

to something we did or said yesterday and say that this action is definitely the cause for what we are experiencing today. Karma operates over many different lifetimes, and for us to experience a karmic effect there must also be appropriate conditions for the karma to come to fruition. All we can say for certain is that if we engage in positive, skillful actions, since they are the cause of happiness, we will definitely experience their result, which is happiness. If we then engage in negative, unskillful actions, which cause suffering, we will definitely experience their result, which is

GREEN TARA

Green Tara, the goddess of mercy and compassion, who holds a blue lotus in each of her hands.

suffering. But we cannot know what karma will ripen at what time or when it will meet the appropriate conditions to come to fruition.

Looking at how karma operates over different lifetimes helps explain some apparent discrepancies we might see in the world around us. Consider the man who, throughout his life, has always been very kind to people and animals. He has largely refrained from negative behavior and may be considered, on all counts, a good man. Then, late in life, his business collapses, his wife leaves him for someone else, and he experiences much suffering. From the point of view of one lifetime, this seems unfair. However, if we consider that in a previous lifetime, even one lived thousands of years ago, this man was habitually cruel to other people and beat his wife, we can see he created the causes for his present experience of suffering. It is possible that, because of his positive behavior in this lifetime, the karmic consequences he is experiencing are less severe than they would have been if he had lived a bad life this time also.

The fact that we have been born as humans at all, which is considered in Buddhism to be "precious human rebirth," is due to our positive actions in previous lives. For karma to ripen, for

it to come to fruition, it also needs appropriate conditions. We can call our previous good actions the principal cause of our precious human rebirth, and our parents a circumstantial cause, which assisted the karma to bear fruit.

This is similar to the flowering of a daffodil; the principal cause of the daffodil flower is the bulb, and the circumstantial causes include soil, fertilizer, water, and sunlight. This demonstrates that particular causes give rise to particular effects; for example, a daffodil bulb cannot produce a tulip plant.

LOTUS

Detail of a painting of White Tara, showing the leafy stem that supports her lotus throne.

Although we are responsible for creating and experiencing our own karma through our actions, nonetheless we do not live in a vacuum, and we are surrounded by other people. In fact, we all live completely interdependently with each other. We can see this from the point of view of karma; if we wish to create good karma by being kind, we need a recipient for our kind act.

His Holiness the Dalai Lama often says that a good heart is the source of all happiness. Not only do we feel satisfaction from being kind and generous to someone, but that person has offered us an opportunity to create good karma for ourselves. The other person, of course, benefits from our act of kindness, and is, therefore, also more likely to act kindly toward others. Cultivating a good heart is a major cause of happiness.

Because we are social creatures and live in society, interdependently, we rely on other people for our existence. For example, we need farmers to grow and harvest food, truck drivers to transport it to grocery stores, shopkeepers to display and sell us the food, and so forth. All events and situations in life are so intimately linked with other people that one person cannot act without depending on and affecting others.

This means that we cannot be happy in isolation, and that if we are searching for happiness ourselves, then everyone else is also seeking the same happiness. Thus, we should also try to help others find happiness as much as ourselves, as our own happiness will partly depend on it.

So how do you proceed to find real, lasting happiness? First of all, you need to let go of the idea that things and experiences can make you happy. Imagine that you are in a beautiful place by the sea, with lovely weather, in a luxury hotel with everything you want within reach. This might

THE MAHASIDDHA LUIPA

The Indian Mahasiddha and Tantric master, Luipa, the "fish gut eater."

make you feel great if your mind is already relaxed and untroubled. But suppose, while you are there enjoying yourself, you receive a phone call telling you that your close friend has died; how can these things still make you happy? The simple answer is they can't, because they never made you happy in the first place; they simply gave you temporary pleasure. This shows how hollow desire is.

Once you have accepted the idea that the things you desire do not provide lasting happiness, you can look to karma for answers. The law of karma shows you that the way to achieve happiness is by engaging in positive actions and refraining from negative ones. Not only do you yourself create the cause for your future happiness, but, by being kind, ethical, and compassionate toward others, you make yourself feel good about yourself while making those around you happy, too. This makes the people who receive your kind actions more likely to respond in a similar manner, which will generate more happiness generally. Obviously, this is a utopian vision of an ideal scenario. Problems and troubles will still constantly arise, but, by not responding negatively, and by continuing your positive behavior, you will avoid creating negative karma, the cause for future suffering.

Happiness is a state of mind, not dependent on wealth, objects, and pleasant surroundings. For instance, rich people suffer, therefore money obviously does not produce happiness. Famous pop stars sometimes have great personal problems with drink, drugs, or failed relationships, all of which are reported avidly in the newspapers.

From this, we may deduce that the so-called desirable situation of having fame and wealth does not, in itself, cause happiness. Conversely, someone who is poor or blind or in a wheelchair may be full of joy. A situation that we imagine would cause continuous suffering may have disadvantages, but it does not stop people from finding happiness.

Ultimately, we are responsible for our own happiness. Once we have learned about karma, and believe it to be true, we can try to live better lives, and happier ones, too, because living a better life actually means living a happier life, while at the same time creating the causes for our future happiness. Buddhist teachings in general, especially those on karma, can guide and support us with methods and advice on how to avoid actions that cause suffering and seek out ones that cause happiness.

love

Restraining yourself
And loving others
Are seeds that bear fruit
In this life and beyond.

Nagarjuna

WISH-FULFILLING TREE

The wish-fulfilling tree (Parijata), the divine tree of the gods
that fulfills all desires.

Usually we only think of love as romantic love or love for our family and friends. From the Buddhist perspective,

love is the wish for all beings
to experience happiness.

By cultivating an all-embracing love in our hearts, we can spread happiness to many other people. When people are happy, their hearts open and they respond more lovingly to others. So, approaching others with love in our hearts means they are likely to respond in a loving manner to us.

MANIDHARA, THE JEWEL HOLDER

Detail of a painting of Thousand-armed Avalokiteshvara, showing one of his attendant bodhisattvas, Manidhara.

This helps create a generally happy environment. The love that wishes happiness for others also creates the karmic cause for the happiness that we will experience in the future.

The cool

waters

of love

extinguish

the blazing fires

of hatred and anger.

There is a Buddhist prayer that includes the line:
May all living beings have happiness
and the causes of happiness.

This is the heartfelt wish that all people and creatures may cause happiness for themselves by creating wholesome karma.

The prayer is called the Four Immeasurables. The immeasurables are virtues, like love, which are so powerful that their effects cannot be measured. By quietly reciting this line to ourselves, we strengthen our wish for everyone to experience happiness. This then becomes an expression of all-encompassing love, which opens our hearts toward others so that we may give and receive love freely.

Karma operates over many, many lifetimes. To give you an idea of what this means, Buddhist teachings suggest that you reflect upon the idea that all beings have, in one lifetime or another, been your mother.

Because everyone you meet has at one time been your mother, an appropriate response is to feel love for these people. This doesn't mean that you should become sentimental or emotional; you need only experience what this thought inspires within you. So when you encounter someone who is making life difficult or unpleasant for you, if you reflect that this person was once your loving mother, it will be easier not to respond badly to the person's current negative behavior.

Concern for others' happiness

Loving-kindness is the genuine feeling of concern for the happiness and well-being of others. We must first develop loving-kindness toward ourselves, as sometimes we feel we don't deserve to be happy, or we judge ourselves harshly. Loving and accepting ourselves is the first step toward developing loving-kindness toward others.

Although we may not like, much less feel love toward, everyone we meet, we can at least try to be kind and courteous to those people we don't instinctively like. We can reflect that these people are also looking for happiness and trying to avoid suffering, just like ourselves. In this way, although we still may not like them, it is easier to act pleasantly toward them and to avoid creating any negative karma.

Developing the habit of being kind and loving toward others creates the karma for us to find love and happiness ourselves.

CLOUDS AND BILLOWING CLOTH

Detail of a painting of the female Mahasiddha Manibhadra, the "mad princess."

Metta is a Pali word
meaning "loving-kindness"
or "friendship." It is part of the living
tradition of Buddhist
meditation practices that cultivates
spaciousness of mind
and openness of heart.

Sharon Salzburg

SODASHRI YANTRA

Yantra of the Indian Mahavidya goddess Sodashri, composed
of intersecting triangles, an eight-petaled lotus, and an outer
square palace with four doorways.

Love is not attachment

It is easy to confuse love with attachment. If you truly love someone, you will want that person to be happy, whether or not their happiness depends on you. Attachment to someone is not a complete expression of love. It demands that another person loves you in return for you loving them. This is trying to make someone else responsible for your own happiness, rather than accepting the responsibility for it yourself. The clinging nature of attachment is unwholesome and can lead to the creation of negative karma.

MACHIG LABDRON

Machig Labdron (1049–1129), the Tibetan yogini who revealed the Chod or "cutting" practice for severing strong attachments.

Love seeketh not itself to please
Nor for itself hath any care,
But for another gives its ease
And builds a Heaven in Hell's despair.

William Blake

As long as we actively discriminate between those we love, those we hate, and those we feel indifferent to, we will not really understand what love is. True love is not preferential.

Love is a bottomless well in our hearts.

One day a group of monks had gone into the forest to meditate according to the Buddha's instructions. The first monk started to feel afraid when night fell and he couldn't see. The next monk heard animals crashing through the trees and felt great fear, while another was frightened about bandits, and another started to feel lonely and afraid. They went to the Buddha for advice. The Buddha told them to practice loving-kindness meditation in order to open their hearts and counteract their various fears. By opening themselves to the world without being preoccupied with themselves and their feelings of fear, they could experience the world and everything in it as benevolent and no longer feel afraid. The practice of loving-kindness counteracts fear.

Loving-kindness helps us recognize and value people for who they really are, stretching beyond our projections and fantasies. Pure loving-kindness is when everyone appears equally dear to us.

Love is an outward movement from the heart that impels you to break out of narrow self-centeredness and open up to the whole world.
Loving-kindness reminds you that acceptance is at the root of love.
It is about gratitude for life, for your own existence, and for other people, without whom you would be alone.

Martine Batchelor

YESHE TSOGYAL

Detail of the Tibetan Yogini, Yeshe Tsogyal, the consort of Padmasambhava.

True love is given willingly
with no expectation of return.

Developing a loving attitude toward those we feel indifferent to or dislike is difficult. However, if we reflect on the nature of friendship, it becomes easier to practice cherishing others.

Consider your best friend. There was a time in your life when this person was unknown to you, and you had no idea that a friendship would develop. Perhaps you had a dear friend earlier in your life who moved away or with whom you had a disagreement that ended your friendship. You might have an old girlfriend or boyfriend whom you once loved very much but who now means nothing to you. Therefore, friends can become enemies, and people we are indifferent to can become friends, and so it is advisable to cherish everyone as a dear friend.

When someone is kind to you, it is easy to feel love for that person in return. When someone is unkind to you, it is difficult to feel love in return. However, cultivating a loving response to others at all times, whatever their attitude toward us, creates the karma that results in us receiving love and happiness in the future. Generating in your heart the wish for all beings to be happy develops loving-kindness.

Being in love

Sexual love is a special kind of love we share with someone. Being in love makes us vulnerable and highlights our emotions, so we need to be especially careful to behave in a manner that will contribute to both people's happiness. An important point for reflection is to check if our partner's happiness is as important to us as our own. If not, we run the risk of acting in a way that may create negative karma and suffering.

When you first feel sexual attraction to a person, ask yourself if this is someone with whom you can develop a loving relationship. If not, you run the risk of being unskillful and causing suffering to yourself, or the other person, or both of you.

We can regard the cultivation of loving-kindness as being like a stone thrown into a pool. As the ripples extend outward in a natural progression to the edges of the pool, so too does our loving-kindness extend outward from our friends and family to acquaintances, on to those to whom we feel indifferent, and eventually even to those whom we dislike.

When you are physically attracted to someone, can you look beyond his or her appearance and reach out to love the whole person?

Martine Batchelor

THE MAHASIDDHA GHANTAPA

The Indian Mahasiddha Ghantapa, the "holder of the bell,"
in union with his consort.

If someone looks at you with an affectionate smile, it makes you feel happy. Conversely, if someone scowls at you angrily, it makes you feel uncomfortable. Your own observation will teach you that everyone wants to experience loving-kindness from others; no one wants to experience anger from others. This is an inspiration and encouragement to practice loving-kindness toward others and to remember to smile.

Pure love
shines like the sun,
everywhere and impartially.

The benefits of love

If we frequently reflect on the benefits and advantages of love, we can develop a good understanding that practicing love and loving-kindness creates wholesome karma for ourselves. This frequent reflection on love also makes our minds familiar with love, so that when negative emotions arise, we dislike them and are less likely to express or act upon them.

By extending our love to include our natural environment, we learn to respect the trees, plants, and animals that make up our world and to try not to harm them.

Everyone needs friendship and love. Going through life with an open mind, a warm heart, and a kind spirit creates the conditions for love and happiness for ourselves and for all those we meet.

Love opens doors;
anger locks them shut.

Love is a fire so powerful
that it will never be extinguished.

KURUKULLA

Kurukulla, the red subjugating goddess of love and desire, who holds the flower attributes of a bow and arrow, noose, and hook.

Love is wanting others to be happy.
It is a natural quality of mind,
but until we develop it
through meditation and other practices
it remains limited,
reserved for a few select individuals.
Genuine love is universal in scope,
extending to everyone, without exception.

Kathleen McDonald

SAMANTABHADRA

The primordial or Adi Buddha, Samantabhadra, the "all good."
He is naked, dark blue in color, and sits in sexual union with his
white consort, Samantabhadri.

Whatever one does
must emerge from
an attitude of love
and benefiting others.

Milarepa

FACE OF VAJRASATTVA

Vajrasattva (Dorje Sempa), the white bodhisattva of purification
and "Lord of the Mandala," in union with his red consort,
Dorje Nyenma.

action and
stillness

Karma comes from the root *kar—*
to do, to make, to act,
and thus means deed, action.

Nyanatiloka Mahathera

THE WHITE SYLLABLE "A"

The syllable "A" is the first letter of the Sanskrit and Tibetan
alphabets, and symbolizes the aspect of "speech" and the
essence of perfect wisdom.

The irrevocability of our actions
implies that we are responsible
not only for our conduct in this life
but for the
impact of our actions
after our death.

Stephen Batchelor

LANDSCAPE AND AURA

Detail of a painting of an offering goddess, depicting
clouds, mountains, swirling silk, and part of her rainbow aura.

As we have seen from the introduction, karma means action, and each of our actions will eventually produce an effect. Good actions produce good effects and bad actions produce bad effects. There are occasions when an action might produce only negative consequences, when nonaction—or being still—is a more appropriate response to the situation.

When you are in the iron grip of anger or hatred, you feel at the mercy of these negative emotions raging through your mind and body. You may think of applying the antidotes of love, compassion, generosity, and so forth, but feel unable to do so immediately. The most skillful thing you can do in these circumstances is to find time and space to be alone, and to practice nonaction till the negative feelings subside. This will save you from yourself and from bad behavior caused by your anger that you will regret later. By doing this, you will protect your happiness and save yourself from experiencing future suffering.

You may think it is beneficial to act upon your feelings immediately, but without reflection actions can destroy happiness. This is not to say that spontaneity is unskillful. However, it takes at least a split second to check whether your action will produce happiness or suffering, so it is definitely a worthwhile habit to develop.

> The art of listening to others
> helps us realize
> we don't need to say
> everything that comes
> into our minds.

Once you have done something, you cannot undo it; the karma has been created and you will experience its effects in the future. That is why it is important to think before you act and to censor your negative behavior, so lessening the suffering of others and yourself now and in the future.

When someone shouts at you, you are under no obligation to shout back.

Action and stillness

Playing with young children is a good way to learn about action and stillness. A child makes it clear when she wants your help or when she simply wants you to notice her doing something. If you respond inappropriately, the child lets you know at once. You can try to adopt a similar attitude of assessing when it is beneficial to join others in some activity and when it is best to rest in stillness. This ensures that when you do join in, your actions will lead to happiness as much as possible.

Meditation is a good way to learn about stillness and how to accept it. Once you have meditated for a while, you start to notice that people often act for the sake of it, because they are nervous, or even because they are afraid of stillness and nonaction. Acting for the sake of it is often unskillful and creates dissatisfaction, so try to abandon actions that are simply something to do and do not lead toward happiness.

In modern society, people are obsessed with changing things, but change is often not for the better. Sometimes it is, in fact, for the worse. Unless you see clearly that changing something will further the cause of happiness, then it should be left alone.

Many of our actions are in response to someone else: Someone speaks, so we answer; someone offers us something, so we accept it. Usually we respond in the same manner as the person who initiated the chain of action, so if someone is kind to us, we tend to be kind back; if someone is offensive, we are tempted to be rude in return.

Karma is not the same as destiny.

It's not fate.

Even though most of

what happens to us is created

by causes from the past,

it is how we respond that will create

what comes into our karmic path

in the future.

Tenzin Palmo

MANJUSHRI

The orange form of the bodhisattva of wisdom, who holds aloft
a wisdom sword in his right hand and a lotus bearing the text
of the Perfection of Wisdom in his left hand.

However, every time we respond to someone or something, we create karma. So we can try to be skillful in how we respond to others by realizing that our responses are actions that will cause certain effects.

The Buddhist teachings actively encourage the practice of harmlessness, which is the pinnacle of nonaction. Not harming people or animals we don't like or feel indifferent to is a form of love and compassion that respects the wishes of others who are trying to find happiness. Simply refraining from harming them in any way is a positive step toward not creating negative karma.

Meditation on harmlessness

Try this tomorrow morning. Take five minutes of your time before starting the day's activities and meditate, calmly watching your breath come and go.

Then, resolve to practice harmlessness today, by being mindful that refraining from action may sometimes be the best thing to do in your circumstances. At the end of the day, recall how many skillful "nonactions" you managed.

Think before you speak. Consider the impact of what you have to say on those who will hear you. Make sure that what you say is worthwhile, and that your words will spread harmony and happiness.

When, just as I am about to act,

I see that my mind

is tainted with defilement,

at such a time

I should remain

unmovable,

like a piece of wood.

Nagarjuna

Nonaction allows us to withdraw into our own meditative inner space. This is where we can find the wisdom to discover when and how to act.

The poet T. S. Eliot wrote about "the still point of the turning world" in his poem "Burnt Norton," one of the famous "Four Quartets," which describes how life is always in flux, constantly moving and changing. When we find this still point in ourselves, we can rest from the ceaseless movement that surrounds us, so, when we do move, our actions will be inspired by stillness.

Because we all share the desire for happiness and want to lead happy lives, it is important to recognize that each person has the opportunity to create the causes for happiness right now. So we need to be vigilant and careful about when and how we act in order to make full use of every opportunity to create lasting happiness and therefore avoid future suffering.

When you see someone in danger or in trouble and spontaneously respond from a feeling of compassion for the person, your action is wholesome and will create positive karma. Even though you may not recognize your action as skillful, it is, nonetheless, a cause for future, lasting happiness.

A purely good action is motivated by
whether it will be of benefit for others,
as well as oneself, and will lead to
happiness for everyone.

If you cannot behave in this skillful manner in a
situation, then it might be better to do nothing.

Life just is,
without us having
to do anything about it.

The results of our actions are themselves the signs of whether we are creating the karma that leads to happiness or to suffering.

The wise person who understands the law of karma avoids any negative actions and adopts purely positive behavior, knowing when to act and when to be still.

It is much more important to examine your own actions and to notice where you can make improvements in yourself rather than criticizing the actions of others.

There is a time and place for every positive action when it will be beneficial and will create the karma for happiness. Look at every situation you encounter carefully in order to know whether it is the right time and right place to do or say what you want to.

The mind that is free from the delusions of desire, hatred, anger, and ignorance knows instinctively when and how to act for the greatest good. Therefore, cultivate a mind that is free from these delusions, in order for happiness to blossom.

LOTUS AND AURA

Detail of a painting of Green Tara, showing a pink lotus above her rainbow aura.

Actions which lead not to distress,
but to a heart bright and cheerful,
are good kamma.
Knowing what kamma is useful,
one should act quickly thereon.

The Buddha

AMITABHA BUDDHA

Amitabha, the Buddha of "infinite light," and the Lord of the
Padma or Lotus Family. He is red in color and holds an alms
bowl in the gesture of meditation.

generosity

The sage does not hoard.
Giving his all to others
he is the richer for it.

Lao-tzu

THE MAHASIDDHA ACINTA

Acinta, the "woodcutter," was one of the eighty-four Indian
Mahasiddhas who revealed the Tantric teachings.

One of the major karmic contributors to your own happiness is being generous to others. Generosity includes an attitude of mind as much as the giving of material objects, time, and attention. Cultivating a generous state of mind, as well as practicing acts of generosity, creates the causes that will eventually result in happiness.

The spirit of giving

In Buddhism, generosity is called dana, and means giving or charity. More specifically, we can say that dana is the spirit of generosity coupled with actual acts of giving. Generosity is, therefore, intimately linked with karma, because acts of generosity are wholesome and positive and cause beneficial effects. Neglecting generosity when we have the opportunity to give can also generate an effect, but this is unskillful behavior that leads to suffering.

The pure gift of giving seeks no reward or return.

Giving expensive material gifts with a mean, closed mind is not really being generous, but offering a wild flower, plucked with a pure heart and given with love, is true generosity.

Give material benefit as you can afford to give it. Generosity must be realistic to be skillful. If you give so much that you then cannot look after yourself, this does not cause happiness for yourself or for those who must then look after you. However, we can usually give a little more than we think we can manage, and this extra effort is important, too.

Giving too much of yourself to others in your personal life or through some caring, helping

THE BLUE LOTUS OF COMPASSION

Detail of a painting of Four-armed Avalokiteshvara, the bodhisattva of compassion, showing the blue night lotus (utpala) that he holds in his left hand.

profession can lead to burnout. Then you are no longer able to work for the benefit of others and can no longer create the positive karma that will cause you to experience happiness. You must take care of yourself in order to be able to continue giving energy and goodwill to others.

If you give a gift because you have to, or it is expected of you, and this is the spirit in which you approach choosing, buying, and giving the gift, then it is not real generosity. At times like these, pause. Think about the wonderful opportunity you now have to practice true generosity and realize that if this is your motivation, the karma created by your action of true giving will lead you toward happiness.

Meanwhile, the sincerity of your action will shine through and the person receiving the gift will also receive the spirit of generosity.

The smallest gift given purely with love creates more happiness than an expensive gift given resentfully, or with the expectation of receiving something in return.

Even if we are materially poor, there are still many things we can give and be generous with. Time is a precious commodity in our modern world, and giving someone the gift of our time can be as precious as a gift of wealth. Giving our time to others often means listening. If we do not give our full attention to others when listening to them, we are also not giving purely.

In the same way, giving a material gift carelessly or resentfully is not generosity. The wholesome karma caused by generosity is considerably less if the spirit of giving is absent from the act.

It is not what we give that is important. It is the mind, or mental attitude of generosity, that is the essence of giving.

Try to give others gifts they will appreciate.

Giving refuge

The Buddha said that one of the things we can offer others is safety or refuge. This means creating a safe environment for ourselves and others. It also includes the idea of actively saving people and animals from danger. When people in Buddhist countries want to practice generosity, one of their customs is to buy an animal, fish, or bird that is destined to be killed, and then to release it. These precious gifts of life and freedom generate much wholesome karma.

Giving material aid to others satisfies their needs and is, therefore, also the gift of happiness.

Dana, giving or generosity, is more or less a basic stance toward others in society, an attitude of generosity, which can be based on goodwill, compassion, or gladness, through giving as an act of encouragement. Generally speaking, although giving refers to material things, it can also be the giving of knowledge or labor.

Bhikkhu Payutto

HEVAJRA

Hevajra, the "joyful vajra," is one of the main meditation deities of the Highest Yoga Tantra traditions. He has eight faces, sixteen arms, and four legs, and embraces his consort Nairatma, meaning "no-self."

Wealth is a result of generosity,
whereas poverty
is a result of avarice.

Geshe Rabten

MONKEY OFFERING SWEETS

Detail of a painting of Ganapati (Ganesh), showing a monkey
offering sweet milk balls, known as laddu.

Generosity is a powerful antidote to attachment and greed. By taking every opportunity that arises to practice generosity, gradually you will begin to develop a giving mind. Transforming attachment into generosity lessens negative karma and leads to the causes of happiness.

Not all acts of generosity are skillful. If you give damaging substances, such as tobacco, to another person, you are contributing to the cause of the person's ill health as the result of smoking the tobacco. Acts of giving harmful things to others are mistakes and not pure generosity. They will create unwholesome karma, and do not lead to happiness, either for yourself or for the recipient of your unskillful gift.

It is easy to give with an unwholesome attitude. For example, next time a beggar on the streets asks you for money, examine your reaction. Most people turn away and choose not to give at all. Not giving is appropriate if you don't have spare change, or feel that you'd rather give to an organized charity than a street beggar. Nonetheless, the beggar is a human being with feelings and needs, and even if you choose not to give, you can be polite and not make the beggar feel bad. If you decide to give something, try to do so with kindness; a few words of encouragement or a smile can make the beggar feel just as happy, if not more so, than a few coins. Giving skillfully creates more positive karma than giving resentfully, or not at all.

Receiving is part of giving, and it is important that we learn to be skillful in how we receive the gifts of others.

Even if you are given something you don't want or like, try to be gracious in the receiving of it, and thank the person wholeheartedly. Remember, by accepting the gift, you are giving the person an opportunity to practice generosity; this is a positive act that will lead to happiness, both for yourself and for the giver of the gift.

Give gifts that you feel will be appreciated,

not those that only make you

feel good about yourself.

Watch your motivation next time you give a present to someone. Do you have the hope and expectation of getting something in return? If so, try to let those feelings go. Expectations often lead to disappointment and negative feelings, which will negate the positive karma created by the act of giving.

When a mother feeds her baby, she offers her milk with love and kindness and with no other desire than to make her baby content. This is a wonderful example of pure generosity.

One of the things we can give is our knowledge or wisdom, which can be of much benefit to others. However, we must be careful only to give these when asked. Otherwise, we may just be trying to demonstrate how clever we are. This attitude of pride can cause negative karma, and does not contribute to happiness.

Once there were two brothers who shared the family farm. One brother was married with a family. The other was single. The single man often thought of his brother, and how, with his wife and children, he would need more than his half of the farm proceeds. Secretly, at night, he would go to the barn and move a few sacks of his own grain to to his brother's side. The married man often thought how his brother must be lonely, and that, if he had a little extra money, perhaps he might find a wife and settle down. He, too, secretly moved a few sacks of his grain to his brother's side from time to time. Neither brother could ever work out why he had more grain than he thought, yet both felt blessed and happy.

When you give material things like money, goods, or services, what is your intention? Often the subtext is that you expect something in return—if not something concrete, at least gratitude. Notice if you are offended when you give something and are not thanked for it.

Martine Batchelor

NAGARJUNA

Nagarjuna was a great second-century philosopher and Indian Mahasiddha. He is depicted here receiving the Buddha's teachings on the Perfection of Wisdom from a serpent spirit or naga.

Love, compassion, and wisdom

If you give the gifts of love, compassion, and wisdom from your heart, your generosity will bear the fruit of happiness.

The best generosity is thinking your friend's needs are higher than your own.

We must give from our hearts as well as our pockets for the act of giving to be complete.

Even if we cannot give material help to those in need, by thinking about them with kindness and compassion, rather than scorn or blame, we develop the mind of generosity.

LOTUS BLOSSOMS

Detail of lotuses and leaves within the aura of a bodhisattva.

No one who has been generous
has ever perished in destitution.

Ibn'Arabi

VASUDHARA

Vasudhara is the goddess of wealth, prosperity, and fertility. She
is golden yellow in color, with three faces and six arms.

Acts of generosity carried out secretly or anonymously ensure that your motivation is not to receive praise and gratitude, or to expect something in return.

Practicing generosity enables you to experience happiness and joy in the present, because you see the results of acts of giving.

This helps transform your concern with your well-being into concern for others. Transforming your self-cherishing attitude contributes to your own well-being by creating the cause for you to experience happiness in the future.

THE GODS SHIVA AND VISHNU

Detail of a painting of the Buddhist tantric deity Hevajra, showing the Hindu gods Shiva (left) and Vishnu (right) being trampled under his feet.

One should give even a single coin
or a single blade of grass of resources;
it causes roots of goodness in this age
and other ages to sprout.

Dogen Zenji

LOTUS, AURA, AND LANDSCAPE

Detail of a painting of Green Khadiravani Tara, showing lotuses,
leaves, and part of her aura and landscape background.

cause
and effect

Karma is often called the law of cause and effect, and it can be referred to as the law of causality. It works in a sophisticated way, beyond the simple concepts of "good actions cause good results" and "bad actions cause bad results." By looking at cause and effect in different ways, we can discover what the causes for authentic happiness really are and put them into practice.

One of the most important things to remember is to look at what effects our actions will cause before we carry them out, so that we can avoid actions that may cause us future suffering.

SHRI YANTRA

Yantra or diagram of the Mahavidya goddess Shri, which is composed of nine intersecting triangles that create a configuration of forty-three separate triangles.

As mentioned in the introduction, we create karma with body, speech, and mind. Mind, or the thought process, is the most important, because you usually have an intention or motivation before you act, and you have many thoughts that do not lead to action. According to the law of cause and effect, skillful thoughts benefit the mind and psyche, while unskillful thoughts harm them.

By cultivating positive thoughts
you create the cause for a happy,
peaceful state of mind.

Reflect upon the fact that the results of your actions in a future life arise from the quality of mind developed in your present life.

The law of cause and effect is not a bank account of credits and debits—you can't really perform good deeds as an investment for the future. Ideally we avoid unskillful actions and cultivate skillful ones because we understand this causes happiness for ourselves and others, now and later.

Simply having the intention to do good is often not enough. We need to ensure that our good intentions give rise to positive actions. Actions that are wholesome and have good underlying intentions certainly cause the effect of happiness.

Desire is our enemy

Desire and attachment can only cause mistaken actions, which create dissatisfaction.

Desire and ignorance are our enemies. They cause us to act selfishly for worldly gain.

Buddhist teachings

encourage us to cherish others

more than ourselves.

ACALA (CHANDRAMAHAROSHANA)

Acala, the Immovable, is one of the ten great wrathful deities of the mandala. He is dark blue in color and holds a sword and a rope noose. He is embraced by his consort.

For the modern Westerner, the teaching
of kamma offers a path of practice
based not on fear of a higher authority,
nor dogma, but rather founded on a clear
understanding of the natural law of cause
and effect as it relates to human behavior.
It is a teaching to be not so much believed
in as understood and seen in operation.

Bruce Evans

CLOUDS AND MOUNTAINS

Detail of a painting of the Mahasiddha Jalandhara, showing the
background detail of clouds and mountains.

If all our actions are motivated by mindfulness, they become the cause not only for the happiness of others, but for our own happiness, too.

Once a monk went to visit his teacher, but his teacher could not see him immediately, so he went to an inn to wait. The maid at the inn did not know that a monk must not drink alcohol or eat meat and must be celibate, and she wanted to seduce him. The monk resisted her advances, but as she kept on offering herself, as well as meat and drink, he wondered what to do. Eventually he thought that if he had one drink she would go away. However, one drink caused his mind to lose clarity, so he had another drink and succumbed to the maid's desires. Then they felt hungry, so they killed a goat and ate it. In this way, the monk broke all of his vows.

The moral of this story is that losing clarity of mind can lead to moral downfall, and that one unskillful action easily leads to another, causing much suffering.

Try this. Remember an instance when something you didn't want came into your life. Perhaps your boss was unpleasant to you at work, your car broke down, or you got sick. Remember your reactions. Usually we hate unpleasant incidents and don't want to accept them, so we fight against them. However, this is aversion, which will simply cause more suffering and do nothing to help. Next time something doesn't go your way, try to accept it; don't fight against it. Although this may not lessen your anguish immediately, it will not increase it and won't create further negative mental karma. Remember everything is impermanent and will eventually pass.

Always be mindful and aware of your intentions. In this way, you will reach an understanding of how intentions lead to habits and how habits influence your experiences in life.

If you encourage skillful actions by developing wholesome intentions, this will produce the effect of happiness.

When we experience happiness, we can reflect that we created its cause. This is an inspiration for good action, as we wish to continue being happy.

Try to keep your mind free from the mental afflictions of desire, ignorance, and anger, as these lead to unskillful actions and suffering. Caring for the happiness of others and doing what we can to help them find happiness lessens our self-concern. When we are less obsessed with our own personal well-being, this naturally causes happiness to arise.

Demonstrating cause and effect

The law of cause and effect is a completely natural, inescapable law of the universe. Buddhist teachers traditionally demonstrate this with the analogy of throwing a stone into a pond.

When the stone is first thrown in, it creates ripples that spread outward till they reach the edges of the pond. This then causes the ripples to spread back to their cause—the stone—and the stone is then subject to pressure from the ripples.

In the same way, our actions reverberate outward, but eventually, when the appropriate

WATER AND ROCKS

Corner detail of a painting of White Tara, showing a rock formation in front of a lake.

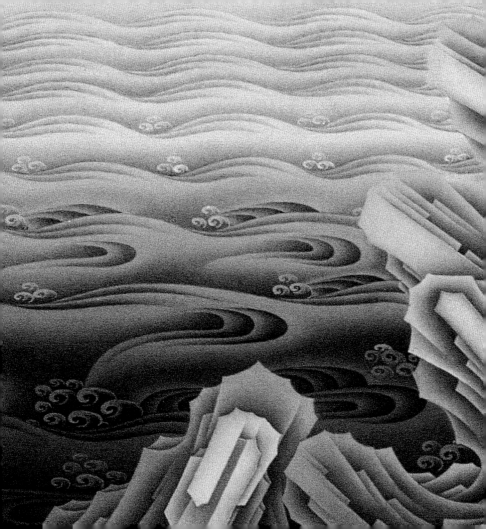

conditions are present, the results come back and we feel their effect.

If we want happiness, we must create the causes for it.

A seemingly well-intentioned action can easily be spoiled by ulterior motives, or by negative mind-states like anger or hatred. The results are then tainted. So it is important to consider your intention before you do something to ensure that the effects of both the intention and the action itself will be positive.

Rather than gossiping about others and saying unpleasant things about them, it is important to think of others kindly and always wish for their well-being and happiness. If you cannot find something nice to say about someone, it is always best to say nothing at all. Such skillful behavior prevents bad karma arising.

As the birds come to roost
in the evening,
so our actions will bear fruit
when the time is right.

Look after your actions, keep them free from anger and craving, and then their results will ripen accordingly. By practicing meditation regularly, we train the mind to be calm and clear. This creates the cause for skillful action, and as a result the mind is filled with peace and joy. Wholesome thoughts and intentions, wholesome speech, and wholesome actions can only bring happiness in their wake.

The Buddha once said:

There is no way to happiness—

happiness is the way.

This cryptic comment indicates that happiness begets happiness, and that, if we endeavor to cultivate both a happy mind and wholesome actions, together they will result in further happiness.

Reflecting on the meaning of cause and effect helps us understand how our actions will affect our experience of life. This helps steer us toward actions that will produce happiness.

All beings are the
owners of their kamma,
heirs of their kamma,
born of their kamma,
related to their kamma,
and supported
by their kamma.

The Buddha

THE MAHASIDDHA SHANTIDEVA

Shantideva was one of the eighty-four Indian Buddhist Mahasiddhas
who lived between the eighth and twelfth centuries. He is shown
levitating as he delivers a discourse on the Buddha's teachings.

living in the
present

Despite our karma stretching over many lifetimes, we can only live in the present moment, and it is important to not get lost in nostalgia for the past and hopes for the future. How we experience the present moment is the result of our previous actions and the cause of the way we experience the future. Therefore it is important to live life in the moment as it unfolds and to experience happiness here and now, rather than to be distracted by memories of happiness or future possibilities. Be here now! Otherwise life will pass you by.

SARASVATI

Sarasvati is a goddess of wisdom and learning, and the consort of Manjushri. With her four arms she holds a lute or vina and a rosary and religious text. Her vehicle, a swan, lifts its wings before her.

Living in the present

Many people have a tendency to daydream; they fantasize about themselves as the heroines or heroes in their own personal dramas, in which they create the illusion of happiness for themselves. However, while dwelling in an ideal scenario that will probably never happen, they miss living their life in the present. In this way they miss any real happiness that might be happening in the present.

Being distracted from the present moment by thoughts and daydreams can lead to mistaken actions. But focusing on the here and now means you have some control over your actions and that you can choose to behave skillfully, which will lead to happiness.

You may think your life is boring, but it's the only one you have right now. So it is best to make the most of it by being present in each moment.

Don't be so busy working hard
for money for your future that you
forget to enjoy life now.

Although making preparations for your future and learning from past experiences are sensible activities, they must be balanced with living in the present. Happiness, like all emotions, can only really be felt in the present moment.

The past is over. You will experience the results of whatever karma you have created in due course. So it is important to make sure that you create positive karma now, so that you can be happy in the present, knowing that you are creating the cause for future happiness, too.

Linear time of past, present, and future is a convenient fiction we use to measure out our days. But all you can really say for certain is,

I am alive now.

Reminding yourself of this helps you live your life fully and well.

Calmly watching your breath enter and leave your nostrils is a form of meditation that will help you be more in touch with the present. In the same way, observing thoughts arise and pass in the mind helps us experience the passing of time.

When you are fully focused in the present moment, you are aware of your many different actions of body, speech, and mind. Being aware and mindful of your actions will help you to act skillfully so that you create good karma, the seeds of future and lasting happiness.

From moment to moment
we are creating our future.
We are not a ball of dust
tossed about by the winds of fate.
We have full responsibility for our lives.

Tenzin Palmo

CLOUDS

Detail of swirling clouds in a dark blue sky from a painting
of White Tara.

Your life is happening
right now.
Enjoy it!
It won't last forever.

Appreciating life in this moment

A good way to counteract boredom is to remind yourself that each moment you are alive is unique. Make the most of it; don't throw it away by wanting something else instead.

Appreciating all of life's moments, not needing to change them or feel aversion to them, means you will live a happier life.

Try the following awareness meditation. Watch your breath come and go for a few minutes, or until the mind quietens. Now focus all of your effort and attention on simply existing in the present moment. Each time your mind wanders off into daydreams and thoughts, remind yourself to return to the present moment. Acknowledge its unique and precious nature, and feel happy for being alive.

Awareness is the key that unlocks
the door of the present moment.

It is a great gift to be alive,
so wake up to every moment.

In order to live in the present, you must practice letting go of reminiscing about the past, and stop

DEER IN A LANDSCAPE

In Buddhism a pair of deer represents harmony, fidelity, and nonviolence. The deer, which never sleeps in the same place twice, is also a symbol of renunciation.

creating fantasies about the future. The past and future do not exist, so how can they possibly make you happy?

We experience our past karma in the present, and the best we can do when unpleasant karma occurs is to accept it graciously.

However, by living in the present moment with awareness, you can ensure that the karma you are creating right now will be wholesome and will only cause happiness in the future.

If you want happiness in the future, you must remember that the karma you are creating right

DRAGON AND LOTUSES

Detail of a Nepali painting of a female bodhisattva, showing lotus blossoms within her aura and an auspicious dragon outside.

now through your mental attitude and physical conduct is the cause of what you will experience. Thus you must strive to think and act skillfully in the present.

Being mindful of your experiences, as they arise from moment to moment, allows you to observe each sensation purely in a more immediate manner, before they submerge under conceptualizations and interpretations. For instance, when you feel pain, instead of immediately thinking that "this hurts," you can just acknowledge that the pain is there; often pain doesn't hurt so much if you don't expect it to. Being with your experiences from moment to moment can lessen suffering and deepen the simple pleasure of being alive.

Once a farmer was making a poor but adequate living from his small farm. Every day he tilled the land and each year harvested enough for his needs. He lived in the moment of each day as the seasons passed and was a happy man. One day he unearthed a pot of gold. His mind started to race with the possibilities of how he could change his life. His peace of mind evaporated with his growing obsession about his new affluent future. He became so distracted that he slipped down a hillside, lost the gold, and broke his leg. Then he couldn't even make his adequate living anymore and his simple happiness was lost forever.

Death can pay you a visit while you are fantasizing or daydreaming about your future. Whatever you can do that is worthwhile and a cause of happiness, do it now, before it's too late.

An old Sufi proverb says:

If you do not have water, then wash with sand; if you do not have sand, then wash with a stone; if no stone is available, then cleanse yourself with intention so that you approach the moment as free of the past as possible.

In this way you are free to live each moment purely, and act from spontaneous goodwill for the benefit of everyone.

When you live fully in the present moment, you can offer others your full attention and see clearly what is happening. This enables you to respond to people and events free from the veils of daydreams and the wandering mind. This is skillful conduct, the cause for happiness.

To stop and pay attention to
what is happening in the moment is
one way of snapping out of . . . fixations.
It is also a reasonable definition
of meditation.

Stephen Batchelor

URGYEN MENLA

Urgyen Menla, the Medicine Buddha from Urgyen in western India,
is a manifestation of Padmasambhava, the lotus-born master who
brought Indian Buddhism into Tibet in the eighth century.

We can unlock the potential for happiness and satisfaction that lies within each of us by becoming aware of our mental processes and then applying discriminating wisdom to all our actions of body, speech, and mind.

Kathleen McDonald

FACE OF WHITE TARA

Detail of a painting of White Tara, showing her golden crown and her three eyes, which symbolize the purity of her body, speech, and mind.

joyful
effort

Once we realize that everything we are experiencing now is the result of past causes, we can understand that what happens to us now is not so important. What is important is the way we respond to whatever happens, because this will shape our future.

Tenzin Palmo

VAJRASATTVA AND CONSORT

Vajrasattva (Dorje Sempa) is the white bodhisattva of purification. He holds a vajra and bell as he embraces his white consort, Dorje Nyenma.

Joyful effort, or enthusiasm, is the great determination to keep going, even when facing those seemingly insurmountable problems. Traditionally, joyful effort refers to meditation and spiritual practice. For example, when you find it hard to act skillfully with good intentions, you remind yourself of the benefits of creating positive karma, and strengthen your resolve in this way. Following a spiritual path like Buddhism can be difficult, but joyful effort keeps your feet firmly on the path. Joyful effort is also a useful attitude in all life situations and gives encouragement when you feel disheartened.

Happiness sometimes occurs for no specific reason; perhaps just being relaxed in some beautiful, natural setting is enough to make you feel it. However, to ensure your future, lasting happiness you need to create the positive karma to experience it. Joyful effort—which is basically trying hard and finding pleasure in the exertion—is a major contributor to happiness.

We can see joyful effort at work by looking at karma and the common wish to experience happiness and avoid suffering. Once you are aware of the law of karma, that your actions determine your future, then you become inspired to think, speak, and act skillfully in order to create the causes of happiness. However, there will be many occasions when you are tempted to behave badly, even though you know this will only bring suffering into your life at some later date. At such times, you can put joyful effort into practice, strengthen your resolve to act skillfully, and avoid the temptation to behave badly.

Responding with joyful effort when things go wrong is a skillful way to overcome difficulties. When, for example, you slip and hit your knee, it hurts and you feel foolish. But you can make things worse by thinking someone deliberately left out something slippery to cause you harm, or by becoming so self-conscious that you remain upset by the incident long after it has passed. Joyful effort in this case is getting up, thinking about how funny it must have looked to those people standing by watching, and maybe even laughing with them. Then you can let the incident go as soon as possible, get on with life, and be determined not to let what happened affect you adversely.

Whenever you experience difficulties, you should try regarding them as opportunities to learn something. Instead of giving up and feeling glum, you can generate joyful effort to strengthen and help you through this difficult time.

Joyful effort encourages you
to keep trying when you feel
weak and inadequate.

Joyful effort is the greatest antidote to laziness and motivates you to get on with whatever it is you need to do.

There are times when we feel tired and depressed and cannot see a way out of this negative mood. By making yourself practice joyful effort, you can help transform such depression. It isn't easy, but try not taking yourself so seriously. Try to discover something about your situation that you can laugh at. You can generate the effort to do something to take your mind off the depression. Or you can simply sit with the depression and cultivate joyful effort to see the situation through, by embracing and accepting it, and reminding yourself that your depression is impermanent and will eventually pass.

Developing self-confidence and self-belief is not egotistical or arrogant. On the contrary, when you feel capable and strong, you quite naturally perform positive, skillful actions and feel love and compassion for others, which promotes a feeling of well-being. Joyful effort lightens depression and creates the cause that results in feeling happy.

Complacency is the enemy of commitment and resolve. If you really want to experience happiness in the future, you must create causes now, in the present moment.

Remembering to keep generating joyful effort every day prevents complacency from arising, so you can remain mindful of your actions wherever possible. Generating joyful effort every morning is a great way to start the day.

THE MAHASIDDHA NAROPA

Naropa, who lived during the eleventh century, was one of the eighty-four Indian Mahasiddhas. He was the guru of Marpa, the teacher of the Tibetan yogin Milarepa.

Joyful effort gives you the courage
to live life positively and well,
and the humility to
keep learning from the lessons
life throws at you.

When you are meditating, it is easy just to sit there and think your thoughts, rather than keeping your attention on your breathing. Joyful effort is a great friend to all meditators, as it helps them keep constantly vigilant.

CLOUDS AND LOTUSES

Detail of a painting showing rainbow clouds and lotus blossoms above a bodhisattvais aura.

Practicing joyful effort means not giving up good actions when you feel selfish or angry. You can remind yourself that good actions contribute to your happiness, and reflect upon the fact that this is what you want to experience.

Sometimes joyful effort is the courage to ask for help from those you trust and who you know to be wise and compassionate. Although you need joyful effort to realize truths such as karma for yourself, the advice of someone who knows more than you do is invaluable.

As we all wish for happiness, developing joyful effort is important. In order to increase joyful effort, you must frequently meditate and reflect on the good qualities of positive actions, such as how positive actions cause happiness. The more you practice this, the more your enthusiasm to do only good develops.

When you put joyful effort into trying to engage only in skillful actions, even though it is possible you may suffer setbacks such as someone being unkind to you, you will not become disheartened.

The great Tibetan Buddhist meditator Milarepa practiced meditation in some of the most austere conditions. He lived in a cave high in the mountains with few possessions and very little to eat. He is often painted green in paintings, since his skin is said to have turned green because one of the few things he had to eat was nettles! However, Milarepa was so happy with his way of life and so full of joyful effort in his meditation practice that he became famous for composing and singing songs about how wonderful it was to have the opportunity to meditate, even in such a challenging place.

Poverty did not concern Milarepa, because this practice of joyful effort made him happy.

MILAREPA

Detail of a painting of Tibet's most beloved yogin, Milarepa (1040–1123), in his retreat cave.

Joyful effort is perseverance in the face of adversity.

The purpose of joyful effort is not about trying to gain material wealth or benefit. True joyful effort is striving to become free from such worldly attachments, because we know they do not lead to happiness.

We can all try harder sometimes. We can also find more joy in the trying.

LANDSCAPE

Detail of a painting of the Tibetan yogini Yeshe Tsogyal, showing part of her aura, with lotuses and mountains.

When the Buddha died, one of the last things he said was:

Impermanent are all created things.

Strive on with awareness.

The Buddha was referring to the importance of joyful effort, together with awareness, in order to awaken to our true nature and to attain enlightenment.

VAJRA YOGINI

Detail of a painting of the goddess Vajra Yogini, in her form as Naropa's Dakini (Naro Khajoma).

compassion

By gradually developing our mind,
our present limited compassion
will grow and expand
to become great compassion.
This is made possible by
reflecting again and again
on the suffering of others.

Geshe Rabten

FOUR-ARMED AVALOKITESHVARA (CHENREZIG)

The bodhisattva of compassion and patron deity of Tibet.
With his four hands he holds a crystal rosary, a lotus, and a
wish-granting jewel.

Compassion is the heartfelt wish for all beings to be free from suffering. Compassion and happiness are therefore linked inextricably—how can we be truly happy if we see others suffering?

Cultivating a compassionate attitude toward others—helping them when we can and not being depressed when we can't—helps create the positive karma for us to experience happiness now and in future lives.

When we feel the impulse to compassion we want to free others from suffering. However, only when we work toward liberating others from

HAND OF GREEN TARA

Detail of the right hand of Green Tara, which makes the open-palmed gesture of generosity and holds the stem of a lotus.

suffering is this compassion in our minds and hearts put into action. Actions inspired by real compassion create strong positive karma, bring freedom from suffering, and create conditions for happiness to flourish.

Understanding suffering

We don't need to feel sad to be compassionate, and, in fact, being overly emotional is seen as sentimentality, not true compassion. Trying to understand how suffering occurs and finding out what we can do to help is a more appropriate expression of compassion.

Actions motivated only by
genuine compassion
create the cause
for happiness.

The Buddha of compassion

Tibetan Buddhism's many different Buddhas and
divine figures, or deities, are seen in paintings and
statues, which are used for meditation practice
and visualizations. These deities serve to inspire
meditators with their depiction of enlightened,
positive qualities. A popular figure is Chenrezig,

the Buddha of compassion. The Dalai Lama is said to be the living embodiment of Chenrezig, and all his actions arise from his compassion for others. Having a painting, statue, or picture of Chenrezig or the Dalai Lama in your home is a wonderful inspiration for the continuous development of your own compassionate mind.

In order for compassion to flower and flourish in our hearts, we must let go of discriminating between ourselves and others or thinking in terms of "us" and "them." It is easy to act compassionately toward ourselves, family, and friends. However, true compassion is spontaneously feeling like helping people and animals we don't know or regard as strangers, or even those we don't like. If we recall that all beings wish to be free from suffering just as much as we do, this can assist us in developing compassion toward them and acting positively to help them. This creates happiness now and the causes for happiness later and dissolves the discrimination between the self and others.

Intellectual ability and cleverness are not required for compassion. As long as there is clarity and awareness in the mind, then even the simplest person can feel genuine compassion. In fact,

sometimes our cleverness and education can get in the way of the powerful simplicity of these compassionate feelings.

A great Zen Buddhist master was leading a meditation retreat for a group of American students. One student approached him in an emotional state. She told him how she was feeling moved to pity for the suffering of others and wanted to help them. She thought this was a great experience of compassion. However, the teacher pointed out to her that she was simply being sentimental, not truly compassionate.

FACE OF AVALOKITESHVARA

Detail of the face and hands of Four-armed Avalokiteshvara, the bodhisattva of compassion.

Compassion is not pity or sentimentality; it is the spontaneous, natural response of wanting to alleviate the suffering of others.

Truly good karma arises from altruism and through developing kind thoughts toward others, especially acting from goodwill and compassion.

The Buddha described the karma of those who have abandoned killing and are possessed of goodwill and compassion in the following way. Because of the good karma developed and nurtured within these people, after death they will either be reborn in a heaven realm or, if reborn as humans, they will be blessed with longevity.

Thus, it is clear that compassionate action creates the cause to experience lasting happiness in future lifetimes.

If we really want to find true happiness, all our actions should, ideally, arise from skillful mental qualities like compassion.

Compassionate acts of speech are just as important as physical actions motivated by compassion. For example, when someone is distressed and experiencing difficulty, we can speak kind words and offer advice or condolences and generally express sympathy. We also need to listen with awareness and attention so that the person feels heard. In this way, we can help to lessen their suffering.

Compassion helps us lose our self-cherishing by responding to the needs of others. Only when we consider the needs and wishes of others as greater and more important than our own can we truly be said to have awakened the mind of compassion. Actions that are free from self-cherishing create positive karma and therefore lead to happiness.

Compassion for all beings

Meditation can help us to uncover and develop the compassion that already exists within us.

The concentration and inquiry that are required in order to meditate deepen our awareness of the inherent nature of suffering and dissatisfaction that we all experience. From the clarity and understanding that comes with such awareness, compassion for all beings arises spontaneously.

When we reflect on the current state of world affairs, it becomes obvious that we need more compassion in our lives. In economic, ecological, social, and political fields, the world is facing problems and issues that can only truly be solved by its entire population working together. We need to find ways to bring a compassionate attitude into world affairs, to create a world in which everyone is considered equal, and equally important.

Therefore, it is important that we live a life of continual mindfulness and mental alertness, as these mind-states will create the most favorable conditions in which compassion can be present and can grow and develop.

When we look at how karma operates, we see that a compassionate mind and compassionate actions form the basis of our happiness now and in the future. Developing compassion and refraining from harmful actions ensures our progress on the spiritual path and will eventually lead us to enlightenment.

From the point of view of karma, it is especially important to make a concerted effort to practice compassion toward our enemies and toward those most in need—this should include those who are physically and mentally ill and those who live far away.

By overcoming our aversion or indifference to these people and finding real compassion in our hearts for them, we will make our practice of compassion stronger and also more habitual, thus helping to relieve suffering as widely as possible.

Compassion, loving-kindness,

altruism, and a sense of

brotherhood and sisterhood

are the keys to human development,

not only in the future

but in the present as well.

The Dalai Lama

THE MAHASIDDHA MANIBHADRA

Manibhadra was one of the eighty-four Indian Mahasiddhas.
She is shown here flying blissfully through the sky.

Practicing loving-compassion

The Dalai Lama has frequently said:

> If you want others to be happy,
>
> practice loving-compassion.
>
> If you want yourself to be happy,
>
> practice loving-compassion.

This means that when you act compassionately toward others, you find peace, happiness, and joy in your heart, which comes as an immediate result of your actions. You are also creating the positive karma for happiness in future lives.

Compassion is genuine concern about others; the spontaneous response to their suffering. This is a universal feeling that is not dependent on culture or which century you live in. Embracing compassion means developing an attitude of universal responsibility toward others, which also contributes to worldwide happiness.

In all the little moments of your everyday life, you can try to be of benefit to others in both small and big ways. Such actions, done with a good heart, are virtuous and create the cause for your own well-being, success, and happiness. Because these virtuous actions are harmonious with their

results, you create the cause and also experience the effect of happiness.

When someone behaves badly toward you, by shouting angrily or even stealing something from you, how should you respond? If you behave angrily in return or try to hurt your assailant, your actions are unskillful and will create karma of a negative nature. However, reflecting that you are experiencing and, therefore, using up negative karma that you created for yourself earlier in this or previous lives will make it easier for you to refrain from retaliation. Then you can actively

THE MAHASIDDHA VIRUPA

Detail of a Nepali painting of Ganapati, showing the Indian Mahasiddha Virupa being offered wine by a courtesan.

cultivate compassion for the person who has hurt you by thinking about the future suffering they have just created for themselves. You then will see no point in causing that person any further suffering, and your compassion will thereby protect your own happiness.

One way to develop compassion for someone you don't like is to consider that the person is, in fact, your created image—that is, how you think of the person rather than their actuality. You are projecting your feelings of dislike onto this person, but this is not their inherent nature. Reflect that other people love this person.

Once you have dissolved the incorrect feeling that this person is intrinsically unlikable, then reflect that he or she wants to find happiness and does not want to experience suffering. The person has people who love him or her, so that whatever faults the person has does not mean he or she is unlovable. Thinking like this helps you to feel compassion for the person.

We can all be inspired by a mother's compassion as she is spontaneously compassionate to her child.

Trying to be a world savior is a worthy ideal, but unrealistic. You need to know your limits—when you can help and when you cannot. Trying to be compassionate beyond your abilities can be counterproductive, because when you try and fail, you may feel like giving up compassion altogether because it is too difficult. However, helping others with a compassionate attitude, acting from a genuine desire to be of benefit whenever you can, and accepting your limitations when you cannot, is a good way to sow karmic seeds for happiness.

The power of compassion conquers all negative emotions.

HAND HOLDING A LOTUS

Detail of a painting of the Mahasiddha Thaganapa, the "compulsive liar," showing his left hand holding a red lotus blossom with its roots.

Sometimes human beings act through kindness and compassion, giving rise to relief movements and human aid organizations. As soon as kindness enters into human awareness, people will undertake all sorts of works for the purpose of helping others.

Bhikkhu Payutto

MOUNT KAILAS

Detail of a painting of Mount Kailas and the sacred lake of Manasarovar in western Tibet.

Compassion is the source of
nonviolent action, and it brings us
inner strength and mental peace.
These qualities also brings us
more smiles, friendship, and harmony.
So compassion is really
something very precious.

The Dalai Lama

VAJRASATTVA (DORJE SEMPA)

Vajrasattva, the white bodhisattva of purification and "Lord of
the Mandala." He holds the attributes of a vajra and bell.

About the artist

Robert Beer (born 1947), a British artist, has studied and practiced Tibetan thangka painting for more than thirty years. One of the first Westerners to become actively involved in this art form, he initially studied for a period of five years in India and Nepal with several of the finest Tibetan artists living at that time. Since 1975 he has lived in Britain and worked consistently on developing the artistic skills, vision, patience, and understanding of this highly complex subject, as well as the historical and cultural context within which it arises. His drawings and paintings have appeared in several hundred books on Tibetan Buddhist art and religion, and he is widely regarded as one of the world's leading experts on this subject. His publications include *The Encyclopedia of Tibetan Symbols and Motifs* and *The Handbook of Tibetan Buddhist Symbols*.

Over the last ten years he has been commissioning and collecting works by the finest contemporary Nepali and Tibetan artists, and he has also been instrumental in introducing the skills of Tibetan art to some of the most accomplished Indian miniature painters of Rajasthan. The paintings of many of these artists appear in this book, and include the Newar artists Siddhimuni and Surendra Man Shakya, Udaya and Dinesh Charan Shrestha, Lalman Lama, Ajay Lama, Sundar Singhwal, Devendra Singhwal, Samundra Singhwal, Amrit Dangol, Raj Prakash, Amrit Devendra, Kungchang Lama, Ratna Bahadur, and Sundar Shrestha. The Tibetan artists include Chewang Lama, Phunsok Tsering, and the studios of Cho Tsering and Dawa-la. The Rajasthani artists include Babulal and Jai Shankar, both of whom have worked under the supervision of Marc Baudin of Jaipur.

With gratitude
to everyone who helped
bring this book to fruition.

Gill Farrer-Halls

Every effort has been made to obtain permission to reproduce materials protected by copyright. Where omissions have occurred please contact Gill Farrer-Halls, c/o Elizabeth Puttick Literary Agency, 46 Brookfield Mansions, Highgate, West Hill, London, N6 6AT.